COLLECTORS GUIDE

TO

COCA-COLA ITEMS

Photography by Don Miller
Marion, Indiana

Published by
L-W Book Sales
P.O. Box 69
Gas City, IN 46933

D1621861

Eighth Printing
1996

© Copyright 1985
Al Wilson
L-W Promotions

Printed by IMAGE GRAPHICS, INC., Paducah, Kentucky

Table of Contents

Al Wilson

Al Wilson has been a salesman most of his life, and rates a masters in his field. Thirty years ago, he bought his first Coca-Cola tray for $1 – sold it for $20 – and the buyer turned it for $70. His interest peaked. There were no price guides then. Atlanta was part of his territory, and eventually he found an underground store that sold Coca-Cola items. Here he got his first ideas on cost and price. He frequented the Archives, also. Although they had many stories to tell, there was just a whiff of any keep-sakes to exhibit and limited knowledge of their value. Several books have now been written that include most of the rare collectibles we know about today.

SO WHY ANOTHER PRICE GUIDE? Al has bought and sold more original Coca-Cola memorabilia than anyone else, including 90% of the pieces listed in other books. He would rather sell than collect, and has been known to pull a prize from his own collection to sell – just for the thrill of it. This price guide (Vol. 1) will reflect his years of selling in and out of the country to the novice and the entrepreneur.

THE CONFUSION OF GRADING

MINT
New condition, in original wrapper or box, no marks or scratches visible.

NEAR MINT
Might appear to be Mint, but close inspection shows minor marks, a slight tear, small crazing, etc. . . . . usually sold for Mint.

EXCELLENT
Only minor hairline scratches, small chips or marks on edges . . . NO RUST on any part of front item.

VERY GOOD
About the same as excellent, except minor flaking and fading, pin head rust spot, small dent or tear, but not on main part of picture.

GOOD
Small dents, scratches, pitting, fading, rust, crazing could be used as a filler.

POOR
All of the above mentioned faults – a rare piece might tempt one to buy an item in this condition. The value is NIL.

NOTE: I advertise in nine trade papers, and receive a number of calls from people who have a Coke item for sale. High prices are being asked for merchandise that a seller refers to (and I quote) "Really good, almost mint, hardly any dents, just a little rust, etc." PEOPLE DO NOT KNOW HOW TO GRADE. The 6 categories outlined above are confusing. I find "over the phone buying" is safer and more realistic, if a scale of 1-10 is used.

TRAYS
(serving, change and tip)

1901 Change Tray
6" Diameter
$2600.00

1907 Med. Oval
10 1/2" x 13 1/4"
$2200.00

1909 Med. Oval
10 1/4" x 13"
$1600.00

1910
10 1/2" x 13 1/4"
$1100.00

1905 Vienna Art Plate
Frame & Box
Wood, Tin, Plaster
$900.00

1903 Hilda Clark
Tin 15" x 18 1/2"
$4000.00

1913
10 1/2" x 13 1/4"
$950.00

1913 Oval
12 1/2" x 15 1/4"
$1100.00

1914
10 1/2" x 13 1/4"
$650.00

1914 Oval
12 1/2" x 15 1/4"
$900.00

1916 Oblong
8 1/2" x 19"
$600.00

1920 Oval
13 3/4" x 16 1/2"
$950.00

1920
10 1/2" x 13 1/4"
$700.00

1921
10 1/2" x 13 1/4"
$800.00

1922
10 1/2" x 13 1/4"
$700.00

1923
10 1/2" x 13 1/4"
$400.00

1924
10 1/2" x 13 1/4"
$800.00

1925
10 1/2" x 13 1/4"
$400.00

1926
10 1/2" x 13 1/4"
$750.00

1928
10 1/2" x 13 1/4"
$550.00

1927
10 1/2" x 13 1/4"
$600.00

1928
10 1/2" x 13 1/4"
$550.00

1929 (Glass)
10 1/2" x 13 1/4"
$450.00

1929 (Bottle)
10 1/2" x 13 1/4"
$550.00

1930 (Telephone)
10 1/2" x 13 1/4"
$350.00

1930
10 1/2" x 13 1/4"
$350.00

1931 (Rockwell)
10 1/2" x 13 1/4"
$825.00

1932
10 1/2" x 13 1/4"
$650.00

1933 Francis Dee
10 1/2" x 13 1/4"
$450.00

1934
10 1/2" x 13 1/4"
$850.00

1935
10 1/2" x 13 1/4"
$400.00

1936
10 1/2" x 13 1/4"
$400.00

1937
10 1/2" x 13 1/4"
$325.00

1938
10 1/2" x 13 1/4"
$225.00

1939
10 1/2" x 13 1/4"
$250.00

1940
10 1/2" x 13 1/4"
$225.00

1942
10 1/2" x 13 1/4"
$300.00

1941
10 1/2" x 13 1/4"
$250.00

1950's
10 1/2" x 13 1/4"
$100.00

1950's
10 1/2" x 13 1/4"
$100.00

1909 Tip
4 1/4" x 6"
$550.00

1906
Tip – 4"
Diameter
$1000.00

1907 Tip
4 1/4" x 6"
$725.00

1910 Tip
4 1/4" x 6"
$725.00

1913 Tip
4 1/4" x 6"
$575.00

1914 Tip
4 1/4" x 6"
$425.00

1916 Tip
4 1/4" x 6"
$325.00

1920 Tip
4 1/4" x 6"
$425.00

Additional trays not pictured in this book are listed on page 89 with their prices

SIGNS

1914 Paper Sign – Framed
31" x 41"
$4000.00

1907 Relieve's Fatigue Trolley Sign
11" x 20 1/2"
$1400.00

1926 Sign – Coca Cola outlined in green – porcelain
10" x 30" – Rare
$900.00

1932 Sign – 5 Color Porcelain
10" x 30" – $900.00

1930's Sign Porcelain
12" x 31" – $600.00

1920's Sign Mfg. Dasco Tin
5 3/4" x 17 3/4" – $400.00

1932 Reverse Painting Sign Glass
11" Diameter – $550.00

1933 Sign Tin
19 1/2"
Diameter
$550.00

1933 Bottle Sign 5 color Tin
11 1/2" x 34 1/2"
$550.00

1926 Bottle Sign 5 color Tin
12" x 35"
$1000.00

1950 2 Sided Corner Sign Metal
16" Diameter
$300.00

1950 Sign – White Celluloid
9" Diameter
$400.00

1930 Sign
Masonite in Metal Frame – 16"
$325.00

1944 Cheerleader Sign
Cardboard Frame
15" x 27"
$500.00

1935 – 2 Sided Triangle
Sign – Porcelain
$1300.00

1930 Triangle Sign w/ applied bottle
Plywood – $650.00

1940's Sign – Triangle w/
arrow Plywood
$800.00

1930's Sign White Porcelain
18" – $550.00

1950's Cash Register Sign – Glass w/wood base - 11" – $450.00

1960's Sign – Tin
20" x 28" – $225.00

1939 – 2 Sided Sign
Porcelain
25 1/4" x 26 1/4"
$700.00

1950's Sign – Celluloid
9" Diameter – $325.00

Will Return Sign Brass
6" x 6" – $110.00

1950's – 6 Pack Sign – Tin
11" x 12" – $550.00

1950's – 6 Pack Sign – Tin
11" x 12" – $600.00

1932 Sign
Tin – 3 Feet
$1000.00

1950's Convex Sign
Metal - 6 Feet
$550.00

1930's Bottle Sign
Porcelain – 12 1/2" – $250.0

Sprite Boy Booth Light
Plastic - 4 1/2" x 6"
$160.00

1931 Bottle x-mas Sign
Tin Embossed
4 1/2" x 12 1/2"
$450.00

Disc with 50th Anniversary
Celluloid – 9" - $275.00

Sprite Box Arrow Sign
(3 Pieces)
Masonite and Wood – 30"
$750.00

Disc "Delicious & Refreshing 1950's
Celluloid – 9" – $325.00

1930's – 2 Piece Sign – Plywood & Masonite – 8" x 26" each piece – $450.00

1950's Sign Plywood & Masonite – 12" x 16" – $325.00

1927 – 2 sided Arrow Sign, Tin – $800.00

1932 Sign – 5 Color Tin
19 1/2" Diameter
$600.00

1930's Sign Cardboard
12" x 16"
$150.00

1926 Sign Tin
8 1/2" x 11"
$1500.00

1927 Sign Tin
8 1/2" x 11"
$1500.00

1931 Sign Tin
8 1/2" x 11"
$950.00

1950's Clock & Lighted Sign
9" x 20"
$525.00

1950's Motion Lighted Sign Water Falls
9" x 20"
$650.00

1950's Motion Lighted Sign
PAUSE – 9" x 20"
$650.00

1950's Stand Up Lighted Sign –2 Sided – $400.00

1950's – 1 gal. Syrup Can
Metal-paper label
$135.00

1949-1953 Radio
(Cooler Shape) Bakelite – $900.00

MENU BOARDS

Chalk board Menu
Tin – 19" x 27"
$275.00

1930 Menu Board
wood – 13 1/2" x 24 3/4"
$400.00

Menu Mirror Glass
2 1/4" x 3 3/8"
$150.00

50th Anniv. Menu Mirror Glass
2 1/4" x 3 3/8" – $175.00

1931 Calendar Celluloid
2" x 3" – $25.00

DISPLAY RACKS

Wall Sconce Cardboard
9" x 12"
$500.00

6 Rack Bottle Holder – Metal
43" High – $425.00

Bottle Frame (for display)
Metal – 16" dia. x 42" high
Rare – $950.00

1970's Dispenser
White Ceramic
$900.00

Match Strike – Porcelain
4 1/2" x 4 1/2"
$350.00

Padlock Key – Brass
1 1/2" x 1 1/2"
$135.00

1930's String Holder
Tin - 16" High
$650.00

DOOR PUSHES

1. Embossed 1930's porcelain 2 1/4" x 35" $215.00

2. 1950's porcelain 3" x 32" – $235.00

3. 1940's raised letters porcelain, 3" x 31 1/2" $210.00

4. 1950's porcelain 4" x 29 3/4" – $225.00

5. (Silhouette Girl) Metal 3 1/2" x 33" – $250.00

6. 1940's raised letters porcelain – 3" x 31 1/2" – $235.00

7. 1930's porcelain - 4" x 28" – $300.00

8. Raised letter, metal, 1950's, 3" x 40" $225.00

9. 1950's metal - 3" x 6" $175.00

10. Door Pull - metal frame $235.00
    Plastic - $200.00

11. Door Pull 1950's aluminum – $200.00

12. Porcelain push plate 4" x 8" – $235.00

13. 1960's metal - 4" x 8" $135.00

14. 1930's porcelain - 3 1/2" x 13 1/2" – $285.00

15. Porcelain - 4" x 11 1/2" $260.00

16. Porcelain - 4" x 11 1/2" $260.00

CALENDARS

1921 – $1700 (Top)
1962 – $80 (Bottom)

1939 – $450 (Top)
1941 - $350 (Bottom)

1945-$250 (Top) – 1943-$275 (Bot.)   1959-$165 (Top) – 1947-$450 (Bot.)

Additional Calendars listed and priced on page 89

1973 Big Wheel
Red & White Box
Metal – $85.00

1960's Box Car (will go with Coca-Cola Train)
Red & White Plastic – $85.00

1970 Truck
Red & Beige Plastic
$40.00

Metal Craft Truck Rubber
Wheels/Working Headlights
$1000.00

Truck with Fold Down
Sides – Plastic
$350.00

Marx Truck with horn on cab
1950's metal – 12" Long
$475.00

Truck (Hong Kong)
1960's Plastic
4 1/2" Long
$85.00

Truck Zip-A-Long
with Man 1970
Plastic 4 1/2" Long
$40.00

Truck Wind-Up
(Hong Kong)
1970's Plastic
3 1/2" Long
$60.00

V-W Van with Man in Cab
Friction – Tin 8 1/2" Long
$300.00

Truck (Japan)
Friction – 1970's
plastic 4 3/4" Long
$70.00

1. Budgie Truck, metal - 5 1/4" – $325.00

2. Friction Truck (Japan), tin, 1950's 5" Long – $300.00

3. Pyro Truck, plastic, 1940's – 5 1/2" Long – $100.00

4. Match Box Truck, metal black wheels, 1950's, 2 1/2" – $110.00

5. Match Box Truck, metal, 2 1/2" staggered cases grey wheels - $130.00

6. Truck, plastic, 1 7/8" Long – $100.00

7. Match Box Truck, metal, grey wheels, 2 1/2" Long - $110.00

8. Friction truck (Japan), 1950's – Tin 4" Long – $160.00

9. Friction truck (Japan), 1950's - Tin 4 1/4" Long - $150.00

10. Friction V-W (Van), 1950's - Tin 4" Long – $250.00

11. Linemar friction truck, 1950's – Tin 2 3/4" long – $225.00

12. Friction truck, multi-color – Tin 1 3/4" long – $30.00

13. Friction truck (Japan) 1950's – Tin 4" long – $160.00

Van (V-W) 1950's – Tin
8 1/2" – $250.00

Friction Truck Bottles
pull out from sides
1950's Tin – 8" long
$500.00

Friction Truck
1950 – Tin
$400.00

Truck Berliet Stradair
frame metal – 4" long
$325.00

Truck Bedford by Dinky
1950's metal
$325.00

Truck 1970's
plastic - 3 3/8" long
$80.00

Metal Craft Truck
rubber wheels– metal
$850.00

Metal Craft Truck
metal wheels
$850.00

1950's Marx Truck Yellow Metal - $550.00

1940's Smith Miller, wood   Smith Miller Truck, wood
blocks, red metal – $1100.00   blocks – red metal $1000.00

Zip Along Truck – White Plastic – $40.00

1950's Sprite Boy Truck Boxed Yellow Metal – $500.00

1960's Buddy L Truck - Boxed Yellow Metal – $400.00

1960's Friction Car w/box
red & white metal - $225.00

1950's Battery Operated Truck w/box
yellow & white metal – $325.00

1950's Yellow truck, plastic – $200.00

1950's Yellow truck, plastic (open sides) $250.00

1940's Sprite Boy Truck, metal – $500.00

Baseball Bat – wood, 32" long – $115.00

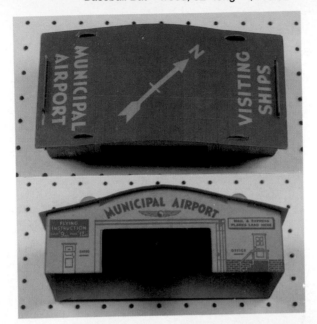

Airport Toy Bldg. 2 pieces, cardboard, yellow & red – $140.00

1930's Bang Gun, cardboard $75.00   101 Magic Tricks $125.00   1932 - 10th Olympiad 2 sides - cardboard, 5 1/2" dia. – $150.00

1930 Yo Yo Edwards Mfg. Co. Cincinnati, OH – wood 1 3/4" – $110.00

1950's Vending Bank w/box, plastic – transparent, 5 1/2" – $260

1950's Dispenser battery operated working cond., tin, 6 1/2" x 9 1/2" – $500

1930's Beanie, felt, 8" dia. – $45

1950's Bank, tin, 2 1/4" x 3 3/4" – $135

Etched mirror w/bottle 1920's glass – 8" x 11 1/2" – $165

Ingot (Cincinnati, OH) 75th Anniversary - Silver – $35

1950's Transistor radio, vending machine, plastic, 2 3/8" x 4 1/2" – $225

Original Stuffed Santa, 1940's, cloth – $165

Buddy Lee Doll (original uniform)
plastic, 12" high
$600 (Composition $800)

1920's Signed property
of Coca-Cola Co.
Leaded Glass Tiffany
type 18" dia. – $4800.

Milk glass shade or globe – 16" dia. – $1250

1920's Bottle Lamp Coca-Cola
Embossed on base glass
20" high – $5000.00

Milk glass shade - porcelain
fixture 8" – $850.00

1920's Gilbert Regulator
Wood – $1900.00

1930's Clock, brass mantle
w/glass dome 6" x 9"
$1100.00

German travel clock
brass – 3" x 3" – $135.00

Round chime clock
oak wood, 15 1/2" dia. – $650.00

1922 – $3700.00

1920 – $800.00

1916 – $500.00

1913 – $700.00

1911 – $500.00

1930's Pretzel Dish – aluminum – $200.00

1930 Sandwich plate, Knowles China Co., 7 1/4" – $275.00

Taylor & Smith & Taylor China Dinnerware
white w/red trim – $260.00 each

ASHTRAYS

1940 Ash Tray w/gold
cig. lighter attached, metal
5" – $110.00

1950's Ashtray tin – 5 1/4" dia. – $25

50th Anniv. Ashtray, metal 3 3/8" sq. –
$40.00

Ashtray w/decals & original matches,
bakelite tray, metal bottle – $790.00

1950's Ashtray (high & low) tin 5 1/4"
dia. – $35.00

Embossed banded dish -
1940's
w/hand holding bottle, metal
4" dia. – $135.00

1. 1920's Cardboard Fan w/1915 bottle – $130
2. Red Cardboard Fan – $75.00
3. 1950 Wicker Fan, Waycross GA
4. 1950's Nude Woman letter opener, plastic, 81/2" long – $160
5. 1935 Pencil box, 10 pieces – $55.00
6. C

7. 1960 Pencil Holder ceramic – $235.00
8. 6 pack bottles cardboard carton – $110.00

OPENERS & CORKSCREWS

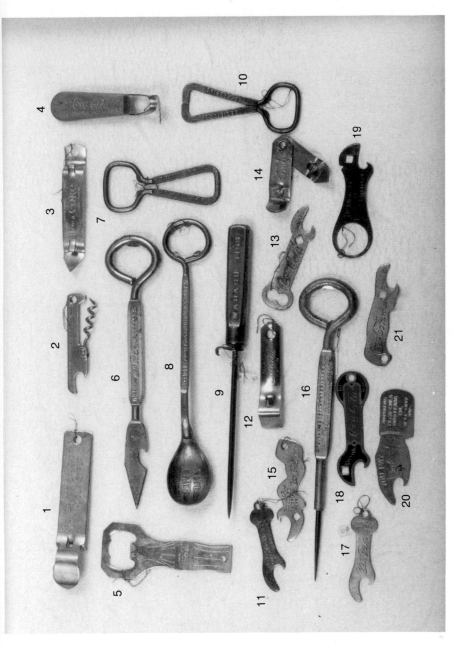

1. $45   2. $70   3. $25   4. $30   5. $55   6. $140   7. $15   8. $155
9. $130   10. $10   11. $35   12. $25   13. $130   14. $20   15. $140
16. $130   17. $55   18. $110   19. $65   20. $165   21. $195

LIGHTERS

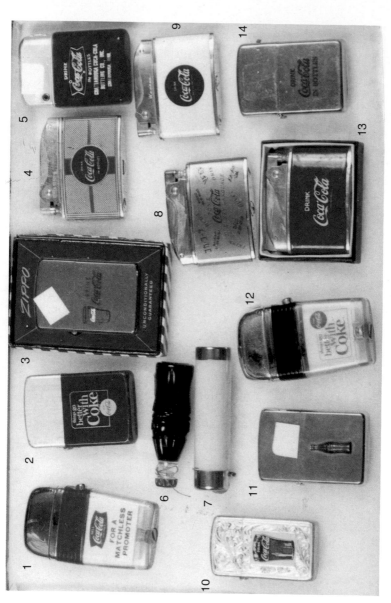

1. 1960's Scripto lighter – $55
2. 1960's Lighter – $45
3. 1950's Zippo lighter in box – $60
4. 1950's Rosen lighter – $80
5. 1960's Chatanooga Btgl. Co. Lighter – $35
6. 1950's Bottle lighter, pull-apart – $25
7. 1950 Dispoz.-A- Lite – $45
8. 1950's Balboa lighter – $55
9. 1950's Lighter – $45
10. 1960's Lighter Par – $25
11. 1960's Lighter Zippo applied bottle – $60
12. 1960's Lighter Scripto – $65
13. 1950's Lighter Rosen – $45
14. 1960's Lighter Supreme – $40

1905 Trade Card or Metamorphic – $700.00

Blotters - (listed left to right; top to bottom)
Row 1: $95, $90, $65   Row 2: $55 ea.   Row 3: $50, $40, $40
Row 4: $40, $65, $25   Row 5: $20, $20, $65   Row 6: $15, $15, $10
Row 7: $15, $15, $10   Row 8: $10, $20, $15

1917 Senate or Act of
Congress Bottle Glass
$170.00

1971 Root Commemorative Bottle
with box and pres. tag - Glass – $500.00

Blue Seltzer, Bradford, PA
glass - $275.00

Green Seltzer, Logansport, IN
glass – $400.00

1971 Display Bottle
w/cap Light Green
Glass 20" – $200.00

1968 Display Bottle
w/cap Clear Glass
20" – $90.00

1960's Display bottle w/cap
plastic brown paint 24" $110.00

Syrup Barrel w/paper label
Wood - 5 gal. - $265.00

1930's Display Bottle
White Chalk 20" high
Pat'd D105529 – $510.00

Pull apart corkscrew - oper
German brass
5 1/2" long – $210.00

Note pad holder w/
music box & pen holder
attached, plastic
5" x 7" – $235.00

1935 Coca-Cola
Glass 3 7/8" high
$55.00

Salesman Sample-Style Cooler
Some are empty, some have
thermos-bottles etc. - red plastic
$135.00

Modified Flare
Glass 1920's
3 3/4" High
$125.00

1934 Salesman Sample
"Open Front" Cooler, metal
8 1/2" x 11" x 9" – $4200.00

"45" Record
"Things Go Better With Coke"
$25.00

"45" Record Holder
red plastic
$55.00

Red metal coke carrier - 1940's
(Rare) – $135.00

Deep yellow carrier coke
decal each end 1940's
(Rare) – $210.00

THERMOMETERS

Thermometer Porcelain
5 3/4" x 18" - $280.00

Thermometer Tin Silhouette Girl
6 1/2" x 16" – $310.00

1960's Thermometer
18" diameter – $225.00

1938 Tin Thermometer
Oval with Xmas Bottle
6 3/4" x 16" - $225.00

1970's Thermometer "Enjoy", 18" diameter - $200.00

Thermometer 1950's
metal 9" – $150.00

1956 Thermometer, metal
Gold Bottle, 7 1/2", $40.00

1950's Thermometer, 12" diameter
$350.00

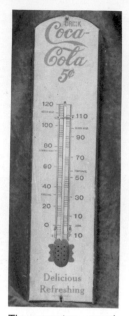

Thermometer Tin Flat
Early 1950's – 17"
$90.00

Thermometer – wood
Circa 1905 - 5" x 21"
$725.00

1930's Thermometer,
Xmas, tin, 17" – $235.00

2 Bottle Thermometer, 1942
tin, 7" x 16" – $400.00

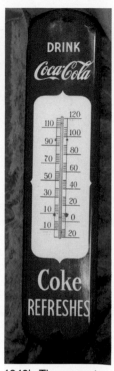

1940's Thermometer
Porcelain 8" x 36"
(Rare) – $500.00

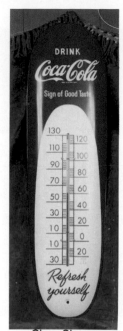

Cigar Shape
Thermometer, metal
30" – $210.00

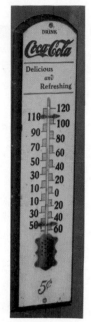

Wood Thermometer
5" x 21" – $725.00

Late 1940's Thermometer
porcelain, 2 1/4" x 9"
$160.00

1945 Thermometer
masonite
6 3/4" x 17 – $300.00

PLAYING CARDS

Silverware by Straus Co.
Richmond, VA & Avon Plate and
Wall Co. – $165.00 each

Paperweight, lucite, 4 3/8" x 4" – $55.00

Paperweight-bottle cap insert, 1960's, glass, 3" diameter – $35.00

Paperweight Spirit of 76, glass, 4" x 3" – $40.00

Paperweight 1950 (Very few originals), glass – 3 1/2" x 2 1/2" – $155.00

Book Mark Owl, Circa 1906
3 1/2" x 1 1/2" - $825.00

Lillian Nordica coupon w/full page. (Full pg. w/ coupon in original magazine more valuable.) Paper 6 1/2" x 9 1/2" – $235.00

Bridge Score Pad, Circa 1944 paper - $28.00

Bound Volume of Pause Books – $20.00

MATCHES

Two Views

1950's Match Book – $3.00   1960's Match Book – $2.00
Match Book - $3.00   1950's Match Book – $3.00
1930's Match Book – $7.00   1950's Match Book – $2.00
1950's Match Book – $3.00   Mid-1930's Match Book – $6.00
1950's Match Book – $4.00   1960's Match Book – $3.00
1950's Match Book – $2.00   1930's Match Book – $12.00
1970's Match Book – $1.00   Pair Dice - $5.00

1970's White Santa
Stuffed Toy
$135.00

1970's Black Skin Santa
Stuffed Toy – $275.00

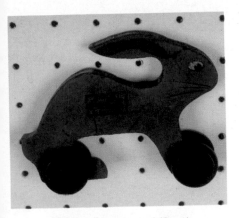

Rabit pull toy – wood (Rare)
3 3/4" x 4 3/4" – $335.00

1940's Lighted Santa Claus
plastic – 17" high – $250.00

1930 Arrow Sign Bottle, metal and masonite,
17" diameter – $450.00

1950's Sign, lucite, 21" x 15 1/2" - $85.00

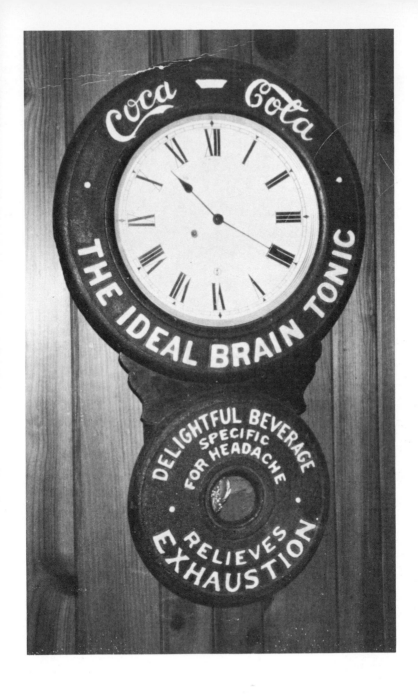

Baird Clock, wood
Circa 1890 – $5000.00

Betty Clock Pendulum Gilbert
Circa 1910 - $2800.00

Electric Clock Recent
Plastic - $45.00

Rocker sign for sidewalk display – 2 sided, tin sign in metal frame
20 1/2" x 33 1/2" – $275.00

Miniature bill board display cardboard sign in plastic frame - $25.00

Sign Fits on top of coke bottle display
plastic, 1950's – $425.00

Santa stand-up display
(many versions), cardboard
6' Tall – $100.00 up

Tin Sign, wood frame, 1935
30" x 72" – $275.00

Straight side bottles each end, 1907
(Rare), tin – $1100.00

Gas today, 1929 tin
27" x 19" – $850.00

1920's Cardboard sign
Approx. 2' x 3' — $850.00

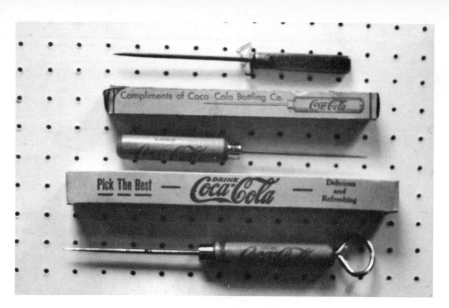

Ice Pick – $40.00
1950's Ice Pick in box, metal w/wood handle - $15.00
1930 Ice Pick-Opener in box - $25.00

Bottle shaped book ends, Circa 1950, bronze – $200.00 a pair

74

1917 Self framed tin sign - 20" x 30" – $3700.00

1904 Hanging sign, 8" diameter
heavy cardboard under glass – $650.00

1960's – 33 1/3 Record, Jonathon Winter and Gene Rayburn – $40.00

45 Record, Eddie Fisher
$30.00

45 Record, Tony Bennett
$25.00

45 Record Andrew Sister
Rum & Coca-Cola – $30.00

1974 Sprite Boy Battery Operated Clock, plastic – $65.00

Sandwich Toaster, Circa 1920's
metal 7 5/8" diameter
$900.00

Carrier for 4 bottles 1960's
cardboard – $25.00

1950's Box of Darts
$85.00

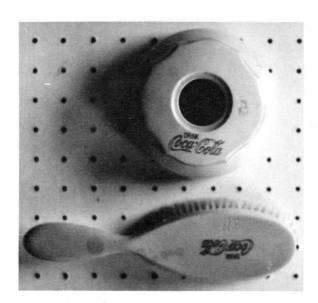

12 Pencil Sharpeners (full) metal in box – $500.00
Circa 1935 Pencil Sharpener, cast iron – $40.00 each

1950's 6 Pack Holder metal – $135.00

6 Bottle carrier – Circa 1935
cardboard – $55.00

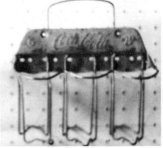

Holder for 6 bottles, 1950's
metal – $160.00

1940's 6 bottle carrier, wood, $70.00

1930's 6 Pack carrier, cardboard
$70.00

1940's bottle carrier divided sections, wood – $155.00

Opener Wall Mount, 1920's – $55.00
Ball cap or hoof shaped – $120.00
Opener Wall Mount – $15.00
Opener Wall Mount Corkscrew – $40.00
Opener Wall Mount Corkscrew and Hook – $80.00
Opener Wall Mount, 1950's – $30.00

1950's Child's Beach Seat
aluminum frame – cloth cover - $80.00

1920's Premix bottle & sleeve
glass – $50.00

1960's Lighted Sign, plastic frame w/ glass face, 8" diameter - $275.00

1970's Hatchet & Knife, 2 pieces, metal in leather case, 10" long – $400.00

1960's Floating fish knife & opener, metal and wood, 11" – $35.00

1940's 6 pack carrier,
bentwood – $130.00

1940's, 6 bottle carrier,
metal – $80.00

1940's 6 pack carrier, aluminum

1950's 6 pack carrier, king size
aluminum – $55.00

1940's 6 bottle carrier, masonite – $60.00

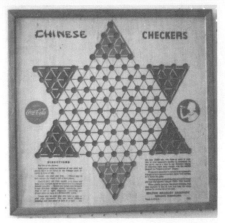

Chinese Checkers Game
(Silhouette Girl) with marbles checker
board - reverse side wood – $140.00

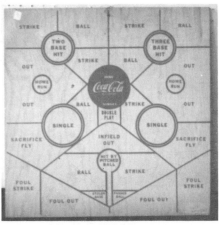

Baseball & Dart Board
Circa 1950, sprite box
reverse wood & cork
$110.00

1935 Dart Board, wood – $85.00

1950's Dispensing Machine in box, plastic – $100.00

Tic-Tack-Toe game in box – $160.00

Winko Baseball game w/box
and board – $275.00

Frizbee in box, plastic – $30.00

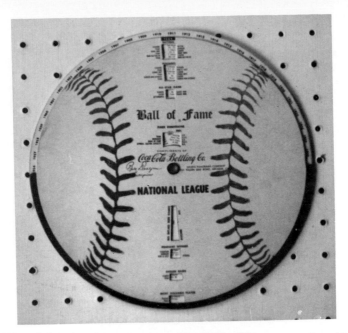

"Ball of Fame" American League on one side, National League on other side
cardboard, 9" – $115.00

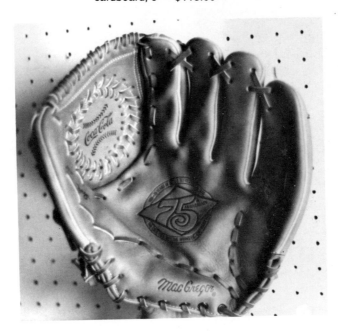

Baseball glove Cincinnati, OH
65th Anniversary, signed by Pete Rose & Joe Morgan
Leather – $250.00

1950's Miniature Dispenser & Bank, plastic - $135.00

1970's Sprite Boy
Domino's, plastic – $25.00

1970's Duncan Yo Yo – $25.00

Yo Yo Memphis, TN – $25.00

1950's Top, Albany, GA - $25.00

1960's Coca-Cola Dispenser in box, plastic – $60.00

1950's Domino's Coca-Cola bottle
embossed on each piece - $60.00

1930's Bingo Card
cardboard - $25.00

Webster's Dictionary
"Little Gem" 1925
leather binding
$55.00

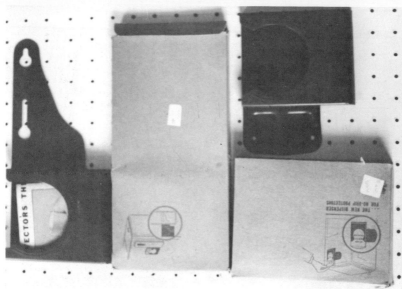

Dry Server Holder attaches to
vending machine, metal – $65.00

Dry Server Holder attaches to
vending machine, metal – $65.00

Thermometer-Barometer,
plastic – $75.00

Inflatable hanging lite, plastic
$45.00

Trays Not Pictured In This Book

1897 – 9 1/4" diameter $8000.00
1898 – 9 1/4" diameter Hilda Clark $8000.00
1900 – 9 1/4" diameter Hilda Clark $7000.00
1899 – 6" diameter $2700.00
1903 – 9 3/4" diameter Bottle Tray $5800.00
1901 – 9 1/4" diameter $4200.00
1903 – 5 1/4" diameter Bottle $4200.00
1903 – 9 1/4" diameter Hilda Clark $4000.00
1903 – 6" diameter Hilda Clark $2500.00
1903 – 4" diameter Hilda Clark $1700.00
1905 – 10 1/2" x 13 1/4" Lillian Russell (Glass) $2500.00
1905 – 10 1/2" x 13 1/4" Lillian Russell (Bottle) $2500.00
1906 – 10 1/2" x 13 1/4" Juanita $1700.00
1908 – Topless $5000.00

Calendars Not Pictured In This Book

1891 – $7500.00	1923 - $850.00	1946 – $250.00	1967 – $85.00
1892 – $7500.00	1924 – $900.00	1947 – $275.00	1968 – $85.00
1897 – $6500.00	1925 – $950.00	1948 – $275.00	1969 – $85.00
1900 – $6500.00	1926 – $900.00	1949 – $275.00	1970 – $30.00
1901 – $4500.00	1927 – $850.00	1950 – $275.00	1971 – $35.00
1902 – $3000.00	1928 – $900.00	1951 – $160.00	1972 – $35.00
1903 – $3000.00	1929 – $900.00	1952 – $160.00	1973 – $35.00
1907 – $3000.00	1930 – $900.00	1953 – $160.00	1974 – $30.00
1910 – $4000.00	1931 – $800.00	1954 – $210.00	1975 – $25.00
1911 – $2200.00	1932 – $550.00	1955 – $210.00	1976 – $20.00
1913 – $1600.00	1933 – $800.00	1956 – $160.00	1977 – $20.00
1914 – $1200.00	1934 – $650.00	1957 – $160.00	1978 – $20.00
1915 – $3200.00	1935 – $750.00	1958 – $210.00	1979 – $20.00
1916 – $1400.00	1936 – $850.00	1960 – $110.00	1980 – $20.00
1917 – $1800.00	1937 – $650.00	1961 – $ 85.00	1981 – $20.00
1918 – $1800.00	1938 – $450.00	1963 – $ 85.00	1982 – $20.00
1919 – $1800.00	1940 - $400.00	1964 – $ 85.00	1983 – $20.00
1920 – $1500.00	1942 – $250.00	1965 – $ 85.00	1984 – $20.00
1922 – $1400.00	1944 – $250.00	1966 – $ 85.00	1985 – $20.00

BUY   SELL   TRADE   APPRAISE

AL WILSON

P.O. Box 33313
Las Vegas, Nevada 89133
Telephone (702) 255-2612

Wilson's

Coca-Cola

Price Guide

A new book by Al and Helen Wilson. A must have reference for all those who are interested in the wondrously broad range of Coca-Cola collectibles! This book is filled cover-to-cover with approximately 2,000 items in color of the most sought-after Coca-Cola products ever made, from advertisements, trays and bottles to haberdashery, jewelry and amazing one-of-a-kind novelties. A useful and gloriously beautiful book!

Al Wilson is the author of *Collector's Guide To Coca-Cola Items Vol. 1 and Vol. 2*. Al and Helen are familiar names to Coke collectors and familiar faces to those who frequent Coca-Cola Collectors Club gatherings. Longtime collectors and dealers, they are experts in the field.

Item #3166 – $49.95 + $2.00 shipping

**1994-95 Values,
254 pages, hardback – 8 1/2" x 11"
2000 Color Photographs of Early to Modern Items**

**INCLUDING:
Advertisements, Trays, Bottles, Jewelry, Paper, Rare Items,
Toys and many more miscellaneous items.**

MAY BE ORDERED FROM

AL WILSON • P.O. Box 33313 • Las Vegas, Nevada 89133

OR

L-W BOOK SALES
P.O. Box 69
Gas City, IN 46933

for **VISA** and **MASTERCARD**
orders only, call:
1-800-777-6450

APPLICATION FOR MEMBERSHIP

Not sponsored by The Coca-Cola Company. Trade-marks used with permission.

The Coca-Cola Collectors Club International (formerly The Cola Clan) is a non-profit organization for collectors (and their families) who are interested in the history and the memorabilia of The Coca-Cola Company.

The Coca-Cola Collectors Club International provides:

- International communication among nearly 6000 collectors
- Markets for buying, trading and selling collectibles
- Informative monthly newsletter with free classified ads for members
- Special monthly merchandise offerings for members
- Regional chapters
- Annual international and regional conventions
- Yearly membership directory

Annual dues for primary membership are $25.00 (in U.S. dollars). Additional members of your family or organization may join as associates to your primary membership for $5.00 per year (an associate member receives all the same benefits of membership as listed above except for the publications of the club). The dues for overseas primary membership are **$40.00** (in US funds) and includes FIRST CLASS postage for the club's newsletter.

The Coca-Cola Collectors Club is not sponsored by The Coca-Cola Company, and is run by unpaid volunteers elected annually from the membership by mail ballot (all primary and associate members may run for elective office).

If you would like to join, complete the form below and return along with one year's dues to:

The Coca-Cola Collectors Club International
P.O. Box 49166
Atlanta, Georgia 30359-1166

- -

PLEASE PRINT **DUES**

NAME (PRIMARY MEMBER)_____ **$25.00**

ADDRESS _____ **($40.00**
overseas)

CITY_____ **STATE** _____ **ZIP CODE** _____

PHONE NUMBER ___(____)_____
area code

NAME (ASSOCIATE MEMBER) _____ **$5.00**
(Give ADDRESS & PHONE if different from primary's)
NAME (ASSOCIATE MEMBER) _____ **$5.00**

TOTAL AMOUNT ENCLOSED _____

If you are already a member, you may use this form for adding associates,
but please do not use this form for renewing your own membership.